Recipes for Cheese Lovers

Recipes Every Cheese Lover Needs

Copyright © 2020

All rights reserved.

DEDICATION

The author and publisher have provided this e-book to you for your personal use only. You may not make this e-book publicly available in any way. Copyright infringement is against the law. If you believe the copy of this e-book you are reading infringes on the author's copyright, please notify the publisher at: https://us.macmillan.com/piracy

Contents

Quattro Formaggi Flatbread 4

Buttermilk Bacon Blue Smashed Potatoes 8

White Pizza Dip 10

Four Cheese Pumpkin Pasta Bake 13

Burrata + Mint 17

Gougères (Traditional Cheese Puffs) 19

Mac + Cheese Stuffed Portobellos 22

Classic Blue Cheese Wedge Salad 25

Baked Chicken Parmesan Meatballs Smothered In Mozzarella 28

Butternut, Mushroom And Fontina Nachos With Crispy Sage 32

Mini Meatball Pizza With Fresh Mozzarella + Roasted Red Peppers 36

Nutella Brie Bites 40

Brazilian Cheese Bread 44

Fried Caprese Salad ... 48

Broccoli Cheddar Casserole ... 51

Cheesy Corn Chowder With Bacon + Gorgonzola ... 55

Beet Ravioli With Goat Cheese, Ricotta And Mint Filling ... 59

Mac 'N' Cheese With Bacon ... 63

Savoury Garlic And Cheese Swirl Buns ... 65

Baked Brie In Puff Pastry ... 68

Fontina, Prosciutto And Sage-Stuffed French Toast ... 70

Melting Cheese And Onion Pie ... 72

Triple-Cheese Crumpets ... 76

California Grilled Reuben ... 79

Quick Croque Madame ... 82

Recipes for Cheese Lovers

Quattro Formaggi Flatbread

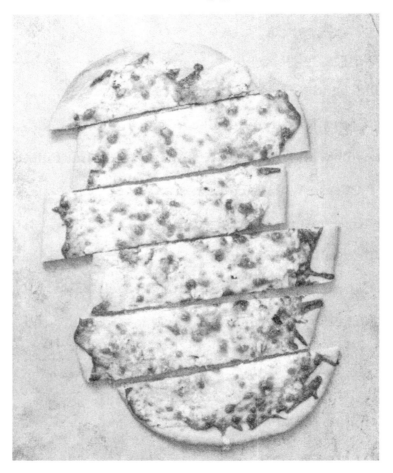

yield: 4 APPROPRIATELY, 2 OBNOXIOUSLY

total time: 35 MINS

INGREDIENTS

1 3/4 cups all-purpose flour

1 teaspoon baking powder

1/2 teaspoon salt

1/2 cup water

1/3 cup olive oil plus more for brushing

2 garlic cloves, minced

1/3 cup ricotta cheese

6 ounces mozzarella cheese, freshly grated

4 ounces parmesan cheese, freshly grated

4 ounces gorgonzola cheese, crumbled

INSTRUCTIONS

Preheat the oven to 450 degrees F.

In a bowl, combine the flour, baking powder and salt, stirring to combine. Add the water and olive oil and mix with a spoon until the dough comes together. Use your hands to finish bringing it together into a ball, then knead it a few times on a floured surface.

Roll the dough into your desired shape — I rolled in into a long oval about 1/4-inch thick — you want it to be thin. Place it on a nonstick (or parchment papered) baking sheet and brush with a bit of olive oil. Bake for 10 minutes, until a few air bubbles form and the dough is golden. Remove the bread from the oven and cover it with the garlic, ricotta (I kind of spread mine out but feel free to do spoonfuls), mozzarella, parmesan and gorgonzola. Return the sheet to the oven and bake for another 10 to 15 minutes, or until the cheese is totally melted, bubbly and golden. Let cool for a few minutes then cut into pieces – however many you'd like!

Buttermilk Bacon Blue Smashed Potatoes

yield: 4 IS EASILY MULTIPLIED

prep time: 20 MINS

cook time: 20 MINS

total time: 45 MINS

INGREDIENTS

2.5 pounds yukon gold potatoes

1/2 cup buttermilk

2 tablespoons unsalted butter

1/2 teaspoon salt

1/2 teaspoon pepper

6 slices cooked bacon, crumbled

4 ounces blue cheese

2 green onions, sliced

INSTRUCTIONS

Wash potatoes and peel or cut off any dark spots or imperfections, leaving as much skin on as possible. Cut into cubes and place in a large stock pot, covering with cold water. Bring to a boil and cook until tender, about 15-20 minutes.

Drain potatoes and place back in the pot over low heat. Add butter and buttermilk, then use a potato masher and mash until your desired texture has been reached. Mash in salt and pepper, then mash in the cheese and crumbled bacon, saving a bit for the top if desired. Taste and season additionally if desired. Top with sliced green onions.

White Pizza Dip

serves about 6-8

INGREDIENTS

1 pint grape tomatoes, tomatoes cut in half

1 teaspoon olive oil

1/4 teaspoon salt

1/4 teaspoon pepper

1 1/2 (12 ounces) blocks cream cheese, softened

8 ounces mozzarella cheese, freshly grated

8 ounces provolone cheese, freshly grated

1/4 cup finely grated parmesan cheese + more for garnish

4 garlic cloves, minced or pressed

1/4 cup freshly chopped basil leaves

2 tablespoons freshly chopped thyme leaves

1/2 tablespoon freshly chopped oregano leaves

crackers, bread or chips for serving

INSTRUCTIONS

Preheat oven to 400 degrees F. Line a baking sheet with aluminum foil then place tomatoes on top. Sprinkle with olive oil and salt, then roast for 20-25 minutes, until bursting. Set aside.

While tomatoes are roasting, mix softened cream cheese with about 7 ounces each of provolone and mozzarella, then and parmesan. Stir in fresh herbs, garlic and roasted tomatoes, mixing well to combine. Transfer mixture to an oven-safe baking dish (mine was 6 x 4 round). Sprinkle with remaining provolone and mozzarella. Bake for 25-30 minutes, or until top is golden and bubbly. Serve immediately with crackers, chip or toasted bread.

Four Cheese Pumpkin Pasta Bake

yield: 12 SERVINGS

prep time: 20 MINUTES

cook time: 10 MINUTES

total time: 30 MINUTES

INGREDIENTS

16 oz whole wheat penne pasta

1 29oz can of pumpkin puree (not pie filling)

1 15oz container of part skim ricotta

1/4 tsp nutmeg

1/2 C pumpkin ale (I used Shipyard Pumpkinhead Ale)

2 tbsp fresh sage, chopped

1/2 lb of Fontina cheese, shredded (I purchased a half pound block from my grocery store's deli department as I've never even seen already shredded Fontina cheese)

1 C part skim shredded mozzarella cheese

1/2 C shredded mozzarella cheese

1/2 C parmesan cheese, divided

2 cloves of garlic, minced

1 C frozen spinach, thawed and squeezed dry

3 tbsp unsalted butter

Salt to taste

INSTRUCTIONS

Cook the pasta until it's reached your desired consistency

In a large pot over medium heat, saute the garlic and spinach in the butter until tender. Add the sage and cook for about 1 minute. Stir in the nutmeg, pumpkin puree, beer, parmesan cheese and ricotta. Mix well. Reduce heat and simmer for 10 minutes. Add salt to taste.

Stir the pasta into the sauce. Pour into a greased 8.5x11 baking dish.

Combine the remaining parmesan cheese, the mozzarella cheese and the fontina cheese. Sprinkle over the pasta.

Recipes for Cheese Lovers

Bake at 350 for 10 minutes. After baking, turn the broiler on low and broil until the cheese is slightly browned.

Burrata + Mint

INGREDIENTS

2 medium heads fennel, cored and very thinly sliced

2 tablespoons olive oil, plus more for serving

6 strips lemon zest, thinly sliced

2 tablespoons lemon juice

8 ounces burrata

1/2 cup fresh mint leaves

Kosher salt and freshly ground black pepper

Grilled or broiled bread slices, for serving

INSTRUCTIONS

Place fennel, oil, zest and lemon juice in a shallow dish; season with salt and pepper. Let stand 10 minutes. (Meanwhile, grill or broil bread slices, if serving.) Just before serving, arrange fennel salad on a large platter. Scatter burrata and mint over fennel. Drizzle with additional olive oil, if desired.

Gougères (Traditional Cheese Puffs)

INGREDIENTS

(makes about 40)

250 ml/ 1 cup water

100 g/ 3.5 ounce salted butter

150 g/ 1 1/4 cups plain flour

180 g/ 2 cups grated Emmenthal or Gruyère cheese

4 eggs

A dash of ground nutmeg

1 egg yolk for glazing

A dash of salt and pepper

INSTRUCTIONS

Pre-heat the over 180° celcius.

In a saucepan, bring the water and butter to a boil. Add the flour, stirring very fast and take immediately off the heat. By now the batter will be roughly in the form of a soft ball. Add the eggs, one by one and stir. It's important to add the eggs slowly – don't worry if it looks too thick, just continue to stir as it will eventually become a smooth batter. Finally add the cheese, salt & pepper and stir to a good dewy batter.

Prepare a baking tray line with parchment paper. You have two choices for preparing the gougères: either put the dough in a pastry bag with a standard tip and pipe walnut sized mounds, or spoon and shape with the help of two teaspoons and evenly shaped ball (again like the size of a walnut). Glaze with the egg yolk for a golden baked finish. Sprinkle the puffs lightly with grated cheese.

Leave an adequate space between each gougères and bake for 25 minutes approx or until puffy and golden. Serve immediately.

ps: You can prepare these in advance and either refrigerate or freeze them. Just take them out again before serving and heat in a high-heat oven for 5-7 minutes.

Mac + Cheese Stuffed Portobellos

yield: 4

total time: 30 MINS

INGREDIENTS

4 large portobello mushroom caps, stems removed

2 tablespoons olive oil

2 tablespoons balsamic vinegar

1/2 tablespoon brown sugar

2 cups leftover macaroni and cheese

2 ounces freshly grated cheese, whatever kind you love

1 green onion, sliced

2 tablespoons chopped fresh herbs

BREADCRUMBS

2 tablespoons unsalted butter

1 garlic clove, minced or pressed

1/3 cup seasoned panko bread crumbs

INSTRUCTIONS

Preheat oven to 400 degrees F.

Heat a large oven-safe skillet over medium heat. Add in the olive oil. Add the mushrooms stem side up and cook for 3 to 4 minutes. Flip and cook for 3 to 4 minutes more. Flip the mushrooms again and add in the vinegar and brown sugar, moving the mushrooms around to coat evenly. Cook for another minute, then turn off the heat.

Scoop a half cup or so of mac and cheese (it can be right from the fridge) into each mushroom cap. Add a little extra grated cheese on top. Place in the oven until warm and the cheese is melted, about 10-15 minutes. Make the breadcrumbs while the mushrooms are cooking, then remove the mushrooms and cover them with the breadcrumbs, herbs and green onions. Serve immediately!

BREADCRUMBS

Add butter to a small saucepan over medium heat and whisk constantly while it bubbles. The minute brown bits begin to form on the bottom of the pan, remove from heat and whisk for an additional 30 seconds. Let butter stand for 2 minutes, then add in minced garlic and whisk. Add in panko and stir well to coat and combine. Set aside.

Classic Blue Cheese Wedge Salad

INGREDIENTS

12 sticks part-skim mozzarella string cheese

1 large egg, beaten

1/4 cup flour

1/2 cup Panko bread crumbs

2 tsp. chili powder

1 tsp. cumin

1/2 tsp. garlic salt

1/4 tsp. oregano

cooking spray (I used olive oil in my Misto)

INSTRUCTIONS

Begin by unwrapping each piece of string cheese, and then cutting them all in half. Place evenly on a plate and freeze until frozen, at least 1 hour.

Preheat oven to 400 degrees F. Line a baking sheet with aluminum foil, and spray lightly with olive oil.

Set up your prep line for the cheese sticks. Fill the first bowl with the flour. Fill the second bowl with the beaten egg. Then fill the third bowl with the panko, chili powder, cumin, garlic salt and oregano, and whisk those five ingredients together until evenly mixed.

Remove the frozen pieces of string cheese, and one by one dunk each first in the flour mixture until evenly coated, then the egg, then carefully roll in the panko mixture. Be sure that all sides of the cheese are coated in breadcrumbs, then gently place on the prepared baking sheet. Repeat with remaining breadcrumbs.

Bake for 8-10 minutes, or until the cheese is melted and just begins to seep out. Remove and serve immediately with your favorite salsa.

Baked Chicken Parmesan Meatballs Smothered In Mozzarella

INGREDIENTS

For the sauce:

1 (28 oz.) can whole tomatoes, liquid reserved

1 tbsp. butter

¼ cup finely chopped onion

1½ tbsp. tomato paste

2 cloves garlic, minced

½ tsp. red pepper flakes

Salt and pepper, to taste

1/3 cup heavy cream or half-and-half

For the meatballs:

½ cup dried panko

1/3 cup grated onion

1 tsp. dried parsley

1 tsp. dried basil

½ cup freshly grated Parmesan cheese

3/4 tsp. kosher salt

¼ tsp. ground black pepper

3 cloves garlic, minced

1 large egg, lightly beaten

1½ lbs. ground chicken

2 tbsp. olive oil

To finish:

4 oz. shredded mozzarella*

2 tbsp. freshly grated Parmesan

2-3 tbsp. minced fresh basil (optional)

INSTRUCTIONS

To make the sauce, add the tomatoes to a blender or food processor. Puree until smooth, adding a bit of the reserved liquid if necessary to smooth the mixture out. Melt the butter in a large, deep skillet or sauté pan over medium-high heat. Add the onion and cook about 1 minute, until it begins to soften. Stir in the tomato paste, garlic and red pepper flakes and mix just until fragrant, about 30 seconds. Stir in the tomato mixture, lower the heat to a simmer, and cook about 5-8 minutes, until the sauce is slightly thickened. Season to taste with salt and pepper. Remove the pan from the heat and stir in the cream. Set aside.

To make the meatballs, combine the panko, grated onion, parsley, basil, Parmesan, salt, pepper, garlic and egg. Stir together with a fork just until blended. Mix in the ground chicken and knead together gently until evenly combined. Form the mixture into meatballs about 1½-inch in diameter.

Preheat the oven to 400° F. Heat the olive oil in a large skillet or Dutch oven over medium-high heat. Add the meatballs to the pan in a single layer (two batches may be necessary if you don't have enough surface area.) Let cook, turning occasionally, until all sides are browned.**

Once all of the meatballs are browned, place them in the pan with the tomato sauce. Sprinkle the mozzarella and additional Parmesan over the top. Bake until the cheese is fully melted and bubbling and the meatballs are cooked through, about 15 minutes. Remove from the oven and garnish with the fresh basil. Serve warm.

*For best results, always use freshly shredded cheese. Pre-shredded cheese comes coated in things such as flour or cornstarch to prevent clumping and results in an unpleasant, gritty texture when melted.

Butternut, Mushroom And Fontina Nachos With Crispy Sage

yield: 4 APPROPRIATELY, 2 OBNOXIOUSLY

total time: 30 MINS

INGREDIENTS

2 tablespoons olive oil

1 small butternut squash, peeled and cubed

1/4 teaspoon salt

1/4 teaspoon pepper

1/8 teaspoon nutmeg

a pinch of cardamom

1 shallot, diced

2 garlic cloves, minced

1 1/2 tablespoons unsalted butter

12 ounces sliced cremini mushrooms, coarsely chopped

8 ounces fontina cheese, freshly grated

6 ounces gruyere cheese, freshly grated

12 to 15 fresh sage leaves

FOR SERVING:

sour cream or greek yogurt

balsamic glaze for drizzling

INSTRUCTIONS

Heat a large skillet over medium heat and add 1 tablespoon of olive oil. Add the chopped squash to the skillet and season it with the salt, pepper, nutmeg and cardamom, tossing well. Cover and cook until the squash is just fork tender, stirring once or twice, about 10 minutes. Remove the squash from the skillet and set it aside in a bowl.

In the same skillet, add another 1/2 tablespoon of olive oil over low heat. Add the shallots and garlic, stirring well and cook for 2 minutes. Add in 1 tablespoon of the butter and once it's melted, add in the mushrooms, stirring to coat. Cook until the mushrooms soften, about 5 minutes, stirring occasionally. Turn off heat and stir in a pinch of salt and pepper. Scoop the mushrooms into another bowl and set them aside for a minute.

In the same skillet, add the remaining olive oil and butter over medium heat. Once it's melted and sizzling, drop in the sage leaves and cook for about 30 sections per side. Remove the leaves and place them on a paper towel until ready to use.

Preheat the broil in you over to the highest setting. I like to assemble the nacho by layering half of the chips, a handful of cheese, some squash, mushrooms, another handful of cheese, and so on until I have 2 or 3 layers. This way it's all cheesy! Pop the nachos in the oven for 2 to 3 minutes, just until the cheese melts and is bubbly and golden. Top with the sage leaves. Serve immediately with sour cream/yogurt and a drizzle of balsamic glaze if desired.

Mini Meatball Pizza With Fresh Mozzarella + Roasted Red Peppers

yield: 1 PIZZA

total time: 2 HRS

INGREDIENTS

DOUGH

1 1/8 cups warm water

3 teaspoons active dry yeast

1 tablespoon honey

1 tablespoon olive oil

2 2/3 cups whole wheat flour

1 teaspoon salt

PIZZA

1/2 batch of bite sized meatballs

1/2 tablespoon olive oil

1 1/2 cups pizza sauce

4 ounces fontina cheese, freshly grated

8 ounces fresh mozzarella, sliced

1 (12-ounce) jar of roasted red peppers, or 2 homemade roasted reds

INSTRUCTIONS

In a large bowl, combine water, yeast, honey and olive oil. Mix with a spoon, then let sit until foamy, about 10 minutes. Add in 2 cups flour and salt, stirring with a spoon until the dough comes together but is still sticky. Using your hands, form the dough into a ball and work in the additional 2/3 cup flour, kneading it on a floured surface for a few minutes. Rub the same bowl with olive oil then place the dough inside, turning to coat. Cover with a towel and place in a warm place to rise for about 1-1 1/2 hours.

While the dough is rising, make the meatballs. Heat a large skillet over medium heat and add the olive oil. Brown the meatballs on all sides, cooking until just browned, about 5 to 6 minutes. Remove from heat and let the meatballs cool a bit.

After the dough has risen, punch it down and place it back on the floured surface. Using a rolling pin or your hands, form it into your desired shape (sometimes I use baking sheets and do rectangles or free form pizzas – this specific dough will yield one pizza large enough to feed about 3-4 people) and place on a baking sheet or pizza peel. Place the towel back over the dough and let sit in the warm place for 10 minutes.

Preheat your oven to 400 degrees F (or if you're using a pizza stone or the skillet method, follow these directions). Spread the sauce on the dough then cover it with the fontina cheese. Add on the meatballs, sliced mozzarella and red peppers. Bake for 30 to 35 minutes, or until the crust is golden and the cheese is bubbly.

Recipes for Cheese Lovers

Nutella Brie Bites

INGREDIENTS

What it took for 13 or 14:

* 1 wheel of brie, cut in half, then rotate the knife to cut into

quarters, then into whatever comes after that, and then maybe two more times, until you get around 14 even wedges

* 1 sheet puff pastry, cut into 14 little rectangles

* 1 egg, lightly beaten

* a few Tbs. of Nutella, slightly warmed so that drizzling is easier

INSTRUCTIONS

Preheat oven to 400.

Lightly coat a baking sheet with cooking spray.

Arrange the pull pastry rectangles on the baking sheet, and lightly brush with egg wash. Place each brie wedge on top of the puff pastry.

Bake for around 20 minutes (maybe 25), or until the cheese has melted all over the puff bites and onto the baking sheet, and they've risen a tad.

Recipes for Cheese Lovers

Drizzle with Nutella and seriously

Brazilian Cheese Bread

Prep time: 5 minutes

Cook time: 15 minutes

Yield: Enough batter for 16 - 20 mini muffin sized cheese breads

INGREDIENTS

1 large egg*

1/3 cup extra virgin olive oil

2/3 cup milk

1 1/2 cups (170 grams) tapioca flour

1/2 cup (packed, about 66 grams) grated cheese, your preference, we get good results with feta cheese (no need to grate), or fresh farmer's cheese (if using fresh farmer's cheese, you may want to add another 1/2 teaspoon of salt)

1 teaspoon of salt (or more to taste)

Special equipment:

One 24-well or or two 12-well mini muffin tins. Mini muffin tins are about half the size of a regular muffin pan. The muffin openings are about 1-inch deep, and 1 3/4 inch wide at the top.

INSTRUCTIONS

Pre-heat oven, prepare mini-muffin tin: Preheat oven to 400°F. Spread a small amount olive oil around the insides of each well of a mini-muffin tin.

Blend ingredients: Put all of the ingredients into a blender and pulse until smooth. You may need to use a spatula to scrape down the sides of the blender so that everything gets blended well. At this point you can store the batter in the refrigerator for up to a week.

Pour into mini-muffin tin: Pour batter into prepared mini-muffin tin, not quite to the top; leave about 1/8 inch from the top.

Bake: Bake at 400°F in the oven for 15-20 minutes, until all puffy and nicely browned. Remove from oven and let cool on a rack for a few minutes.

Eat while warm or save to reheat later.

Note that Brazilian cheese bread is very chewy, a lot like Japanese mochi.

Fried Caprese Salad

INGREDIENTS

1 large tomato - sliced into 3 - 1/2" rounds

salt/pepper

1 cup all purpose flour

1 egg - beaten

1 cup panko bread crumbs

1 cup canola oil

1 Galbani® Mozzarella Fresca - sliced into 3 - 1/2" rounds

6 fresh basil leaves

balsamic cream

INSTRUCTIONS

Season tomato slices with salt and pepper and place onto a plate lined with paper towels. Set aside.

Place flour, egg, and panko into 3 separate shallow bowls for dredging.

Dip tomato slice into flour. Lightly tap to remove excess. Dip into egg and then into panko. Transfer to plate and continue with remaining tomatoes.

Into a medium sized skillet add oil and heat over medium heat. When hot, add tomato slices and cook for approximately 30 seconds on each side OR until golden.

Transfer to a plate lined with paper towels. Season with salt.

To assemble: tomato, mozzarella, 3 basil leaves. Continue with two additional layers. Garnish with a drizzle of balsamic cream.

Broccoli Cheddar Casserole

Prep time: 15 minutes

Cook time: 55 minutes

Yield: Serves 5 as a main course, 10 as a side

INGREDIENTS

2 pounds (900g) broccoli, stems removed (can use vegetable peeler to peel, then slice and eat like celery) and crowns cut into florets (about 8 cups of broccoli florets)

2 strips thick-cut bacon (about 2 ounces), cut crosswise into 1/4-inch wide strips

5 large eggs, beaten

1/3 cup (43g) all-purpose flour

1/2 cup (118 ml) heavy cream

1 cup (236 ml) whole milk

2 to 3 teaspoons freshly ground black pepper (1 to 2 teaspoons if using fine ground black pepper)

1/2 teaspoon salt

2 teaspoons Dijon mustard

8 ounces (225g) cheddar cheese, grated

INSTRUCTIONS

Blanch the broccoli florets: Bring a large pot of salted water to a boil (1 Tbsp salt for 2 quarts of water). Add the broccoli florets and boil for 3-5 minutes or until just tender enough so that a fork can easily pierce the floret, but still firm. Strain and rinse with cold water to stop the cooking.

Cook the bacon: While the water in step one is coming to a boil, cook the bacon pieces on medium heat in a frying pan until lightly browned, but not crisp. Remove to a plate lined with paper towels to absorb the excess fat. Set aside.

Make the egg mixture: Preheat oven to 425°F (220°C). Butter a 2 1/2 quart casserole dish. In a bowl, whisk the eggs into the flour, then whisk in the cream and milk. Add the black pepper (more or less to taste), salt, and mustard. Mix in about a third of the cheese.

Assemble the casserole: Place the blanched broccoli florets in the casserole dish, sprinkling about a third of the cheese over the broccoli florets as you lay them down. Sprinkle the bacon pieces over the broccoli.

Pour the egg, cream, milk, cheese mixture over the broccoli, moving the broccoli pieces a bit so that the mixture gets into all the nooks and crannies. Sprinkle the casserole with the remaining cheese.

Bake for 25 to 40 minutes, or until set. Once the top has browned, you may want to tent with aluminum foil to keep from burning.

Cheesy Corn Chowder With Bacon + Gorgonzola

yield: 4

total time: 45 MINS

INGREDIENTS

2 tablespoons olive oil

4 tablespoons unsalted butter

1 sweet onion, finely diced

2 garlic cloves, minced

1/2 teaspoon salt

1/2 teaspoon pepper

4 tablespoon flour

3 cups chicken stock,

3 cups fresh or frozen sweet corn, I used 8 ears

4 ounces sharp aged cheddar cheese, freshly grated

1 cup half and half

1/4 teaspoon freshly grated nutmeg

4 slices cooked bacon, crumbled

2 ounces gorgonzola cheese, crumbled

INSTRUCTIONS

Heat a large pot over medium-low heat and add the olive oil and butter. Once melted, add in the onions, garlic, salt and pepper, stirring to coat. Cook for 5 to 6 minutes, until the onions softened and begin to turn translucent. Increase the heat to medium and add in the flour, whisking constantly for 1 to 2 minutes until it is evenly dispersed to create a roux. Cook the roux until it is fragrant and begins to turn golden in color.

Pour in the chicken stock, whisking constantly. Add in the corn. Increase the heat to medium-high and stir until the liquid thickens a bit. Bring the soup to a boil and cover, then reduce it to a simmer and let it cook for 10 minutes. Remove the lid and stir in the half and half and the cheddar. Stir continuously until the cheese melts. Add in the nutmeg and taste the soup. Season it additionally with salt and pepper if desired.

Serve immediately with crumbled bacon and gorgonzola on top.

Beet Ravioli With Goat Cheese, Ricotta And Mint Filling

PREP TIME: 3 hours

COOK TIME: 20 minutes

SERVES: 4

INGREDIENTS

For the beet ravioli and filling

2 large beets

Recipes for Cheese Lovers

2 1/2 teaspoons olive oil

2 eggs

3 1/4 cups flour (plus more for dusting)

1 teaspoon salt

1 cup ricotta cheese

3/4 cup goat cheese

1 tablespoon chopped parsley

1 tablespoon chopped mint

1/4 teaspoon salt

1/2 teaspoon black pepper

1/4 cup grated parmesan cheese, plus more for serving

For the brown butter sauce

8 tablespoons butter

3 1/2 tablespoons lemon juice

INSTRUCTIONS

For the beet ravioli and filling

Preheat oven to 400° F.

Wrap the beets in tinfoil and place on a baking sheet. Roast about 1 hour or until the beets are tender.

Remove beets from oven and allow them to cool a bit before handling. Remove the skins, place in a food processor and puree the beets until smooth.

Add eggs to the food processor and pulse until combined. Add flour and salt and process until dough comes together.

Transfer the dough to a well-floured surface an knead until smooth about 7 to 10 minutes (add in more flour if the dough is sticky)

Cover and let rest for 2 hours.

Before dough is done resting make the filling by combining chopped parsley, mint, ricotta, goat cheese, and salt and pepper in a mixing bowl. Set aside.

When dough is done resting, cut into 4 pieces. Roll out each piece to form a thin layer (about 1/8") of dough.

Place 1/2 Tablespoon of filling onto one sheet of the dough about 1/2" from the edge. Continue to place spoonfuls of filling along the dough about 1" from each other.

Place one of the other pieces of rolled out dough on top of the piece with the filling on it. Pinch the dough around the filling to form the ravioli.

Use a sharp knife to cut out the ravioli into individual squares.

Pinch the edges of each ravioli with the edge of a fork. Set aside each ravioli in a single layer on a baking sheet dusted with flour until ready to cook.

Add ravioli to a pot of boiling water. Stir until the water returns to a boil. When the ravioli float on their own, about 5-7 minutes, they are finished.

Serve on individual plates drizzled with brown butter sauce (below) and shaved Parmesan cheese.

For the brown butter sauce

Melt butter in a pan. Cook over medium heat until the butter is completely melted and brown bits start to form.

Add lemon juice, remove from heat.

Mac 'N' Cheese With Bacon

45 Minutes Serves 2 Easy

How do you make mac 'n' cheese better? Add bacon of course! This oozing cheesy pasta bake is also rich with Red Leicester and finished with a crunchy breadcrumb topping. Double up the recipe for a family meal

INGREDIENTS

breadcrumbs 1 handful, fresh and chunky

olive oil

butter 1 tbsp

garlic 1 clove, finely chopped

mustard powder 1 tsp

plain flour 1 tbsp

whole milk 250ml

Red Leicester 100g, grated

rigatoni or other short pasta 175g

streaky bacon 4 slices, grilled until crisp

INSTRUCTIONS

Heat the oven to 200c/fan 180c/gas 6. Put the breadcrumbs on a baking sheet, drizzle with oil, season, and bake for 5 minutes.

Melt the butter in a pan. Add the garlic and mustard and cook for 1 minute. Add the flour and whisk on a low heat for 1 minute. Gradually whisk in the milk, then bring to a boil, whisking. Reduce heat and simmer until thick (about 4 minutes). stir in the cheese until melted.

Boil the pasta until al dente, drain and mix with the cheese sauce and bacon. Spoon into 2 large ramekins. Top each with breadcrumbs and bake for 20 minutes until golden.

Savoury Garlic And Cheese Swirl Buns

1 Hour 40 Minutes + Proving

Makes 7A Little

Effort

If you love garlic cheesy bread then you'll love these super soft savoury swirl buns. Packed with gooey mozzarella, these buns are an ideal side for a dinner party with friends

INGREDIENTS

whole milk 175ml

dried active yeast 2 tsp

caster sugar 1 tsp

plain flour 350g, plus extra for dusting

egg 1, beaten, plus 1 beaten for glazing

unsalted butter 50g, very soft, plus extra for the tin

ready-grated mozzarella 100g

GARLIC BUTTER

unsalted butter 125g, very soft

parmesan (or veggie alternative) 75g, finely grated, plus extra for scattering

garlic 3 cloves, crushed

flat-leaf parsley finely chopped to make 3 tbsp

INSTRUCTIONS

Heat the milk to just below a simmer then cool to warm. Whisk in the dried yeast and caster sugar, and leave in a warm place for 10 minutes or until a thick foam has formed on top of the milk.

Tip the flour into a large mixing bowl and stir in 1 tsp salt. Make a well in the middle of the flour and pour in the yeasty milk mixture, beaten egg and softened butter. Stir until the mixture is combined and comes together into a rough dough.

Tip onto a lightly floured worksurface and knead for 5 minutes until the dough is smooth and elastic. Form into a ball, put in a bowl and cover with oiled clingfilm. Leave in a warm place for 1 1/2 hours.

To make the garlic butter, beat together the soft butter, parmesan, garlic and parsley.

Turn the dough onto a lightly floured worksurface and knead gently for 30 seconds. Roll into a rectangle measuring about 30cm x 50cm.

Turn it so the longest side is nearest to you, then spread ¾ of the garlic butter over the dough, leaving a 1cm border around the edges. Scatter over the mozzarella.

Roll the dough up, starting with the long side closest to you and keeping the roll even. Cut into 7 equal pieces and put cut-side up in a well-buttered non-stick 23cm springform tin. Cover the buns loosely with oiled clingfilm and leave in a warm place for 40 minutes to prove. Heat the oven to 180C/fan 160C/gas 4.

Brush the buns with beaten egg and sprinkle with a little more parmesan. Bake for 35 40 minutes or until deep golden brown. Very gently melt the remaining garlic butter in a pan. Cool the buns in the tin for 15 minutes before releasing, then brush liberally with the melted butter.

Baked Brie In Puff Pastry

1 Hour

Serves 4

Easy

Looking for a delicious and elegant appetiser? This seriously simple recipe features baked brie topped with chutney oozing from golden puff pastry, a crowd pleaser every time.

INGREDIENTS

baby brie or coulommiers 300g (Waitrose does a petit brie)

puff pastry 500g pack (use an all-butter puff for a better flavour)

tomato or shallot chutney 1 tbsp

egg 1 yolk, beaten

salad leaves dressed in vinaigrette to serve

INSTRUCTIONS

Heat the oven to 220c/fan 200c/gas 7. Take the cheese out of the fridge and unwrap it before you start. Cut the pastry in two and roll each piece out on a floured surface, make one about 1 cm bigger than the cheese all the way around and the other slightly thinned and about 3cm bigger than the cheese all the way around.

Put the smaller pastry sheet onto a baking sheet and put the cheese in the middle. Spread the chutney on top of the cheese. Dampen the pastry around the cheese with water. Lay the other sheet on top, smooth down and press the top pastry sheet onto the bottom. Trim around the edge with a sharp knife, leaving a 1 cm-border and rough the sides of the pastry up. Brush with the egg yolk and score lines in a swirling pattern from the centre of the pastry outwards.

Bake for 10 minutes and then turn the oven down to 180c/fan 160c/gas 4 and cook for 20 minutes or until the pastry is golden and puffed. Leave it to rest for 10 minutes before cutting it. Cut into quarters and serve with the salad leaves.

Fontina, Prosciutto And Sage-Stuffed French Toast

20 Minutes

Serves 4

Easy

The ultimate eggy bread. A delicious toasted cheese sandwich. French toast filled with fontina, sage and prosciutto. Whatever you call it, this is a special comfort food recipe for four

INGREDIENTS

crusty bread 8 slices

fontina 300g, sliced

prosciutto 12 slices

sage a few leaves

eggs 2, beaten and seasoned

butter for frying

INSTRUCTIONS

Layer the fontina, prosciutto and sage on 4 slices of bread then cover with the other slices. Dip the sandwiches in the beaten egg, soaking both sides.

Heat a knob of butter in a frying pan and fry the sandwiches on both sides pressing down with a spatula as they cook until golden brown and the cheese has melted. Cut in half to serve.

Melting Cheese And Onion Pie

2 Hours

Serves 8

Easy

Try our seriously indulgent cheese and onion pie. This easy vegetarian cheese pie is the perfect winter comfort recipe to feed the whole family

INGREDIENTS

onions 3-4 large

butter 50g

floury potatoes 400g, peeled, halved and cut into ½ cm slices lancashire cheese 200g, grated

mature cheddar 50g, grated

double cream 100ml

PASTRY

plain flour 150g, plus extra for dusting

self-raising flour 150g

sea salt 1 tsp

butter 150g, chilled and diced

white wine vinegar 1 tbsp

egg 1, beaten

INSTRUCTIONS

To make the pastry, tip the flours into a bowl and mix with the salt. Tip in the butter and squash it into the flour with your fingers, rubbing it together. Stop when you have a mostly breadcrumb texture with the odd lump of butter. Mix the vinegar with 2-3 tbsp of ice-cold water and drizzle over the flour mix, then use a knife to stir in a figure of 8 movement until it starts to clump. Bring together briefly with your hands. Wrap in clingfilm and chill in the fridge for 30 minutes.

Halve and peel each onion, then take off the first layer (you can freeze this for stock). If they are really old onions, take off the second layer as well – the onions need to melt into the sauce and the outer layers of old onions will be too tough to break down. You want to end up with around 450-500g of peeled onions. Chop the onions and add to a non-stick pan with 200ml water and the butter. Put on a lid and simmer for 20 minutes, then take off the lid, turn down the heat and cook until most of the moisture has gone and you have an onion purée that is gently frying in the butter but not colouring (this can take 20-30 minutes, so be patient). Take off the heat, season and cool.

Drop the potatoes into boiling salted water and cook for around 5 minutes, until really soft. They should be really tender but holding their shape. Drain and leave to cool.

Lightly flour the worksurface, then rollout 2/3 of the pastry to line a deep 20cm pie tin, keeping the pastry quite thin. Leave an overhang and then put in the freezer while you roll out the other 1/3 for a lid.

Tip the onions and potatoes into a bowl and add the cheeses and cream. Taste and add a little more seasoning if it needs it. Gently stir together, then tip into the pie dish. Put the pastry lid on top and trim the edges so the bottom and top are the same size, then crimp with your forefinger and thumbs, to seal. Wash with egg, then bake at 190C/fan 170C/gas 5 for 40 minutes until deep golden. If freezing, cool completely, then cover and transfer to the freezer. To reheat, defrost in the fridge overnight, then heat the oven to 180C/fan 160C/gas 4. Unwrap the pie and reheat for 20-30 minutes until piping hot. Leave for 10 minutes before cutting into wedges.

Triple-Cheese Crumpets

1 Hour + Proving + Resting

Makes 16A Little

Effort

How do you make fresh crumpets taste even better? Add three types of cheese, a teaspoon of mustard powder and slather on a good helping of butter of course!

INGREDIENTS

full-fat soft cheese 50g

whole or semi-skimmed milk 200ml

strong white bread flour 300g

caster sugar 1 tsp

dried yeast 1 tbsp

English mustard powder 1 tsp

bicarbonate of soda 1 tsp

strong cheddar 75g, grated

strong red leicester 50g, grated

butter for greasing

INSTRUCTIONS

Melt the soft cheese and milk together in a pan, whisking until the milk is steaming. Take the milk off the heat and stir in 250ml of cold water. Leave until the milk is just warm.

Mix the flour, sugar, yeast, mustard powder and 1 tsp salt in a large mixing bowl and make a well in the centre. Stir in the warm milk, gradually, with a wooden spoon – beating until the batter is really smooth.

Cover with a tea towel and leave to stand (in a warm place) for about 45 minutes until the batter is bubbly.

Mix in the bicarb with the grated cheddar and red leicester, cover again and leave for 15 minutes.

Grease the insides of 4 crumpet rings and a non-stick frying pan generously with butter. Heat the frying pan over a medium heat, then sit the rings in it and quickly ladle enough batter into each to come a third of the way up the sides of the rings. As soon as the batter hits the pan it should sizzle, if it doesn't, turn up the heat slightly. Try not to disturb the batter too much when scooping from the bowl. You want to keep all the bubbles when ladling the batter into the crumpet rings.

Cook for 8-12 minutes until the surface of each crumpet is bubbly and looks completely set (otherwise they will remain raw in the middle). The bottoms should be very deep golden.

Lift off the rings with a couple of forks to help, and turn the crumpets over. Cook for just a minute more until the tops are brown, then lift out, and repeat to use up all the batter. Keep the crumpets on a tray while you cook the rest, then reheat them in a low oven for a few minutes if you want to eat them all at the same time. Eat freshly cooked, or save and toast later.

California Grilled Reuben

15 Minutes

Serves 2

Easy

This West Coast version of a deli sandwich uses smoked turkey rather than pastrami. This makes more coleslaw than you'll need for the sandwiches but it'll keep for 2-3 days in the fridge

INGREDIENTS

carrots 2, finely shredded

white cabbage ¼ small, finely shredded

red onion 1/2 small, finely sliced

white wine vinegar

mayonnaise

large white bloomer 4 slices

sliced smoked turkey 150g

emmenthal cheese 4 slices

gherkins 4, sliced, plus extra to serve

soft butter 1 tbsp

RUSSIAN DRESSING

mayonnaise 1 tbsp

tomato ketchup 1 tsp

creamed horseradish 1 tbsp

INSTRUCTIONS

Put the carrot, cabbage and onion in a bowl. Add 1 tsp of white wine vinegar and 2 tsp of mayonnaise, season and mix together.

Mix the dressing ingredients. Spread the dressing over one side of the bread. Add a couple of tbsp of coleslaw to two slices, then the turkey, then the cheese. Add a few slices of pickle then top with the other slices of bread, dressing-side down. Spread the outside of the sandwiches with soft butter. Heat a large frying pan and fry on both sides until crisp and golden and the cheese has started to melt. Serve with extra pickles.

Quick Croque Madame

30 Minutes

Serves 2

Easy

Croque madame is a classic favourite and this quick version makes for an easy indulgent meal. Ready in just 30 minutes, it's perfect for a midweek comfort food treat

INGREDIENTS

sourdough bread 4 large slices

Dijon mustard

gruyère 100g, grated

thick-cut ham 4 slices

butter

crème fraîche 4 tbsp

eggs 2 small

INSTRUCTIONS

Spread the sourdough slices with a thin layer of mustard on one side, then make sandwiches with half the gruyère and the ham. Spread the outside of the sandwiches with butter.

Heat a non-stick frying pan that will hold both sandwiches and fry them on both sides until crisp and golden.

Mix the crème fraîche and the rest of the gruyère, then spread on top of the sandwiches. Slide under a hot grill until the cheese bubbles. Fry the eggs in a separate pan, then top each sandwich with an egg.

Printed in Great Britain
by Amazon